Samuel Jones Spalding

Sermon Preached in the Whitefield Church

Samuel Jones Spalding

Sermon Preached in the Whitefield Church

ISBN/EAN: 9783337343101

Printed in Europe, USA, Canada, Australia, Japan

Cover: Foto ©Lupo / pixelio.de

More available books at **www.hansebooks.com**

PREACHED IN

THE WHITEFIELD CHURCH. NEWBURYPORT,

BY

REV. S. J. SPALDING, D. D.,

AUGUST 8, 1875,

AND OTHER PAPERS,

IN MEMORY OF FRANCIS DANE.

SERMON.

" Because as the flower of the grass he shall pass away." — James i, 10.

WE are admonished daily of the great uncertainty of everything pertaining to our outward material life. Life itself is uncertain, our health is uncertain, our physical comforts, our opportunities for the enjoyment of friends and associates are uncertain, our property is uncertain, — in fine, all that belongs to us and constitutes the surroundings of our spiritual being is changeable and transient.

My own mind was deeply impressed with this fact the past week while attending the funeral services of a merchant of Boston, whose birth and early business life were in this county, and whose summer residence of late years has been in his native town. Among merchants he was accounted a very successful man, and he had accumulated a large property. Having a great love for rural life, he purchased, some years since, the old homestead of his family, to which, from time to time, he had made important additions. This constituted his farm, which, under his wise care and direction, ranked among the best cultivated farms in Essex County. His dwelling-house was capacious and substantial, but his barns and other buildings were the special objects of his interest and satisfaction. His herds of cattle, his flocks of sheep, his horses, and all his domestic animals were selected from the most improved breeds, and cared for with faithful attention. His implements of husbandry were of the most thorough construction, and of the latest invention. The walls enclosing his fields were evidently built to last for generations. The road which passed his farm was a model of road-making, and indicated, like everything else about his place, the thoroughness of his character.

A few days since the owner of this splendid estate was suddenly struck down by paralysis, and after a brief period of unconsciousness, he passed from earth.

At his burial his house and grounds were thronged by friends and acquaintances. They came not only from his native town and from his place of business,

but from all parts of the county and from many miles away. And it was no formal service which this crowd rendered, nor was it called together by any promise of novelty or display. It was only a quiet country funeral, and in its details just such as the deceased himself would have chosen, marked only by its subdued stillness and the universal expression of deep sorrow.

A sudden death is always impressive; but it was not this fact which drew together that large and sympathetic multitude. So we may well inquire what there was in the life and character of the man who was so much respected by his acquaintances and so sincerely mourned by his friends. Archbishop Tillotson has said, " To commend those excellent persons the virtues of whose lives have been bright and exemplary is not only a piece of justice due the dead, but an act of great charity to the living, setting a pattern of well-doing before our eyes, very apt and powerful to incite and encourage us to go and do likewise."

Francis Dane was born in Hamilton, Mass., Aug. 6, 1819, and was the son of John and Fanny (Quarles) Dane. His father died June 6, 1829, leaving a family of ten children, — six boys and four girls. The estate of his father, which was a

farm of about eighty-five or a hundred acres, when divided, after paying all demands, gave to each of the children $429.00. Mrs. Dane bought out the heirs and retained the farm, with which, and the income of a small store, she brought up her large family. She was a woman of much more than ordinary executive ability and thrift, and it was from her Francis inherited some of those special qualities which fitted him for the successful merchant.

He tried various kinds of labor: he worked for one or two seasons on a farm, he tried the trade of a mason, but nothing which he attempted seemed to furnish the proper opening for his abilities. At last his mother, about the year 1834, gave him four five-dollar bills with which he was to go to Danvers, now Peabody, and purchase leather to be made into shoes and sold. This was the beginning of his career as a shoe manufacturer and merchant, and was the narrow gate through which he was to pass on to success. The results of his first venture were sold in New Hampshire for cash or notes, which his mother, who it seems was his banker, kindly discounted for him, and thus he went on in the business.

It was at this time that he met with John Osborn, Esq., who, in some remarks before the New England

Shoe and Leather Association, on the death of Mr. Dane, gave an account of his early acquaintance with him : —

Mr. President. — It may be proper that I should speak at once, as my acquaintance with Mr. Dane commenced with the earliest period of his business career. About thirty-six years ago a young man of youthful appearance, with a little old horse and wagon and a case of boys' brogans, appeared at my place of business, at South Danvers, and desired me to furnish him leather in exchange for his shoes. I readily consented, and for many months after, he appeared regularly, once a week, with the same equipage and went through with the same ceremony. After a while I suggested to him the economy of bringing two cases instead of one, and his reply was that he could not do it, as he was unable to get them made at Hamilton. I then advised him to move to South Danvers, which advice he soon followed, and then commenced what proved to be his successful business career."

In the spring of 1840, when not quite twenty-one years old, he removed to South Danvers and commenced business as a shoe-manufacturer. By his sterling business qualities he soon made a decided impression among his acquaintances, and no man had warmer or firmer friends. At first his pecuniary success was very moderate. " He once told me," said Mr. John Osborn, " that his progress during the first four years in business was very slow; he hardly realized five hundred dollars net profits over and above actual expenses during all that time." But he saw the possibilities of business, and persevered.

Oct. 10, 1842, he married a lady of his native town, Miss Zerviah Brown. Of his life in South Danvers,

and of the high esteem in which he was held as a citizen, merchant, associate, and friend, all who knew him speak in terms of praise. In 1857 he began business on Kilby Street, Boston, and in 1860 became a resident of that city. He had already established for himself a reputation as a successful manufacturer, and his name had become well known in all the cities South and West. With Baltimore, especially, he had large transactions.

His resources were now so ample that he was able to extend greatly his business, and under his wise management his wealth increased rapidly. Yet he was not without heavy losses, and he experienced the reverses to which all business men are exposed. At the opening of our late war, the indebtedness to him at the South was immense. The crisis called forth all his energy, caution, forecast, and courage. He went through the trial nobly, and came out successfully, but with the loss of nearly eighty thousand dollars.

" I will merely state," said Mr. Thomas E. Proctor, President of the New England Shoe and Leather Association, " what you all know, that, as a merchant, he was energetic, prompt, honorable, sagacious, persistent, successful. As a financier he was almost unequalled. I well remember how he stood during

the first years of the Rebellion, holding an immense stock of unsalable goods. With his pocket-book filled with protested notes he yet continued his large business. Under all these disadvantages, with the business and finances of the country disorganized, his credit remained unimpaired and unquestioned, and I hazard but little in saying he was a lender of money all the time."

This mere outline of the life of Mr. Dane suggests some most useful lessons to our young men.

It is a mistake to suppose that only the learned professions can develop superior intellectual powers. No one more than the true man of business has occasion for strength, clearness, discrimination, and quickness of mind. Let no one imagine that his natural gifts need rust because his circumstances throw him into active, practical life. He will require every mental power in full force if he would understand all the complexities, and be ready for all the emergencies of business.

Intellectually Mr. Dane was endowed with qualities which, from the start, gave promise of large success. He had a very retentive memory which he could trust to an uncommon degree. He carried no memorandum-book, and made few notes of his many and complex transactions in business, and

2

yet no item was ever overlooked or forgotten. He had great clearness of mind, so that matters essentially distinct never became involved in his memory or his plans. This quality was accompanied with the power of prompt decision and energetic, persistent action.

You will notice that he entered upon business with good habits. These he owed very much to the love and fidelity of his excellent mother. In the simple manners of his early home was laid the foundation of that health, vigor, and elasticity of spirits which characterized him as a man of business and an associate. Mr. Dane was not a moody person; one caught the influence of his thoroughly healthy spirit, and conversation with him, even for a few moments, was an exhilaration. He had a strong and constant flow of cheerful, hopeful feeling. His farm, while it gratified a taste for rural life and objects, was a deliberate plan for recreation; and under his practical good sense he made it the means of essentially advancing the agricultural interests of the County and the Commonwealth.

He began business in a very small way. He adapted himself to his necessities, and was not ambitious of display; he had no mean desire to appear any more than he was. In this respect Mr. Dane

was a noble example. He did not follow the mistaken policy of making a large debt the first step towards a large fortune; he never forgot the rule of proportion; he did not undertake a business for which he was unfit, nor incur hazards which he could not measure. By not rushing blindly into risks, he gradually prepared himself to meet reverses when they came.

He was self-reliant; his early circumstances helped to force upon him that independence of spirit which became one of the most important elements of his success. He held this poise of mind without any show of self-conceit, and without any arrogance; yet it was very evident that he had decided faith in himself. His opinions on all matters of business or of politics or of men were emphatically his own. These opinions were not hasty or impulsive conclusions. It was his habit to obtain all possible information from all accessible sources, and to consult freely with his friends and acquaintances; but his own judgment, once formed, could not be easily changed; others might differ from him, but he held firmly to his own views.

enough for my mother, and it is high enough for me."
As he was more than six feet in height, it was evident
that if he found no inconvenience, few others would
be troubled.

There was in his character what might be called
an instinct for thoroughness. Shams in anything
were his detestation. His workmen would sometimes
complain of his criticisms, as though nothing could
suit him: no detail escaped him; he insisted that
every shoe made for him should be the best of its
kind. But his criticism was calculated to make his
workmen feel that they could and ought to improve,
yet without conveying discouragement. His farms,
his stock, his implements of husbandry, in fact, everything to which he put his hand or over which he
could throw his influence, evinced this same love of
thoroughness.

It is noticeable that Mr. Dane identified himself
fully and heartily with the interests of the community
in which he lived. Mr. Abbott, of Peabody, thus
speaks of him : "When here in our village, in every
one of those events which make the history of a place,
he put himself in the van. Scorning every obstacle,
by the magnetism of his own healthy spirit he in-
fused hope and courage in others, strengthened the
weak, emboldened the doubting, and pressed on and

persevered until the end in view was finally accomplished."

The same was true of him when he removed to Boston. He entered with all his heart into the interests of that metropolis; he could not have done more for the promotion of her prosperity and for the building up of her trade had he been a native and a constant resident of the city. He loved Boston, and was jealous of her honor and success. It is a misfortune that numbers regard her only as a great shop in which they can make money.

Mr. Dane was a generous competitor. In all his relations with his associates he was free from petty envy and jealousy. In the world of business, the rivalry is sometimes very sharp and close. Mr. Dane was not a man to disparage the commodities of others with the hope of selling his own, or to speak unfavorably of the character and credit of men of business. He had a large and comprehensive view of trade, and saw clearly that, for his own best success, others must succeed too. He found both his pleasure and his interest in assisting others.

He was a kind and considerate creditor. No man enjoyed making a good sale better than he did; but, unlike many merchants, he made his customers his friends. The men who came to feel the

warmest attachment to him were those to whom he sold largely in trade. The profit he received was but one element of the transaction. It seemed to be an especial object with him to make his customers his friends; hence, in their disappointment and distress, they naturally went to him, and never went in vain. He entered at once into their anxieties, and afforded them all possible assistance. Numbers of men have been indebted to him for timely aid; his sympathy and his help went together.

He was a man of thorough integrity. This was the uniform testimony of all his associates. " He always," said one, " met all his obligations ; his word was as good as his bond, and could always be relied upon." " Mr. Dane," said another, " was a man on whom we could rely. He always said what he meant." From another we learn, " I always found Francis Dane upright in his dealings, and I can truly say that, in my judgment, the trade has been more honorable for his connection with it, and the community has been made better for his having lived in it."

His integrity was more than mere personal honesty, it was aggressive ; he not only kept his own conduct in the line of strict honor, but he insisted that others should keep in the same line as far as all transactions with himself were concerned ; he did not hesitate to

rebuke with due severity any act of meanness or duplicity, even in his most intimate friends and in those older than himself, thus preserving the channels of influence pure.

Mr. Dane was a generous man. Mr. Proctor says of him on this point: —

"We all knew of his generosity upon all occasions, and whatever may have been the standard in former times, at the present time and in this city the best standard the public have by which to estimate the character of men of wealth is the liberality with which, during their lives, they distribute the wealth with which God has endowed them in public and private charities. And, judged by this standard, Mr. Dane stands pre-eminent. Not to enumerate other instances of his liberality, his name has appeared at the head of every subscription paper that has been circulated in our trade during the past twenty years, — or if not at the head, near the head, and for a sum never second to any on the list."

This generosity took with him a most practical turn. He was interested in the parish to which he belonged in Boston, an efficient member of its Finance Committee, and always bore his own share with alacrity. He desired to advance its best success, and gave not only money but time and thought to secure it. He was also very liberal to the little church at Hamilton. He was hospitable, and hospitality in its largest and best sense is but one of the forms of generosity.

"Very many of us," says Mr. Proctor, "have partaken of his hospitality both in city and country.

His house and his table have always been open to his friends and nearly always filled with them, and he never was so happy as when surrounded by his friends and acquaintances."

Another form of this generosity, and one no less commendable, was his great kindness to his large circle of kindred. "He kept," says Mrs. E. C. Cowles, "one or two nieces in our school for a dozen or more years, requiring always that their attention should be confined mainly to practical branches. Several of these thus became fitted for useful positions in society." He also showed his interest in their school, but in so unostentatious a manner that it can hardly be mentioned in detail.

That he had at heart the welfare of his own townspeople appears from the following extract from a letter of Mrs. Cowles : —

"I am sorry that he should have died without making provision for a good business academy in Hamilton, such as he repeatedly told me he desired to establish."

This interest in education appeared also in the Board of Trustees of Dummer Academy. He cheerfully gave much of his valuable time to consult for the interests of that institution, and no one was more punctual at all the meetings of the Board

He had great interest in young men, which was evinced by the fact that he was always accessible to them, and that through his direct influence a very large number obtained good situations in Boston.

No persons know each other better than business men. The ordinary transactions of life in the store, the market, the bank, and the exchange bring out not only the best qualities but the weaknesses of men. And the best test by which a man can be tried is the honest judgment of his business associates. By this standard Mr. Dane was a rare man. H. P. Kidder, Esq., of Boston, writes: —

"In all my long experience with business men, there have been very few who have so impressed me by all the qualities that go to make a true man as Mr. Dane. In all that I have had to do with him, or have known about him, he has been a true friend, always ready to take his share of any burden, and sure to be relied upon for aid on all occasions, not merely as a duty, but also as a pleasure. We shall miss him in our church matters, where we were always sure of his hearty aid and counsel, and the community will miss him as an honest and generous citizen."

Isaac H. Bailey, Esq., of New York, writes: —

"During an uninterrupted friendship of a quarter of a century, I had constant opportunities to test the soundness of his judgment, the strength of his integrity, and the goodness of his heart. He had the happy faculty of assisting his friends by showing them how to help themselves. Everybody who knew him sought his counsel, and always found advantage in following it. He was a kind neighbor, a steadfast friend, and a useful citizen. There are many instances in my memory of his having lifted despondent men out of discouraging difficulties by pointing out methods of extrication which his sturdy common-sense enabled him to devise. And there are not a few instances in which he staked his means most liberally

to relieve men in whom he had faith from pecuniary embarrassments which threatened to engulf them."

His pastor in Boston, Rev. E. E. Hale, writes, after referring to his own personal loss : —

" I have just been saying to a friend that, for many years past, Boston has been much more indebted to Mr. Dane than Boston itself knew; and I am sure that we who were his friends, and know we are, have never met him but to feel that we have been made stronger by his cheerful, hearty spirit."

In this death, there is an impressive admonition to those before me, who are in the fulness of their strength and are bearing the burdens of large responsibilities. Mr. Dane was but fifty-five years and eleven months old when he died. On the 22d of June last I met him on a Board of Trust, and of the nine members present no one seemed to have a firmer hold on life than himself.

Our departure may be sudden. To one looking at the farm of Mr. Dane from the roadside, it was evident that he was in the midst of large improvements. The scarred sides of the gravelly hills which he was removing into the neighboring bogs, the half reclaimed meadows, the partially rebuilt walls, — all showed that his plans ran on far into the coming years. And this was a sensible view of life. It is a great mistake which some men make, to close their business career after they have acquired a competence.

Life is given us for work, not for ease. Look out on nature to-day, and how is every twig and spear of grass and humble plant putting forth all its vegetable energies to reach the ripening of its seeds, to accomplish the end of its being. It were well if this great impulse of nature could quicken man.

As reasonable beings, knowing that our close of life may be unexpected, we are to hold that fact in remembrance; and with all our far-reaching plans of work, have them so arranged that, if need be, they can be taken up and completed by another.

Again, we see the amazing difference there is between character and circumstances.

The large estate, collected by years of toil, self-denial, and the most careful calculation, is already regarded as no longer his. He has passed beyond all interest in his homestead, and all care for his barns, his flocks, and his herds. These were his circumstances, his material belongings; they formed no part of his being. "We brought nothing into this world, and it is certain we can carry nothing out of it." Our circumstances affect us only as they take hold of and control our intellectual and moral being. It is within the power of the will to transmute gold into knowledge by furnishing the means of travel, books, etc.; it can transmute gold into culture by procuring the

best masters and models. — into the highest earthly
happiness by relieving human misery. Wealth, to be
an enduring good, must become the means to a
higher end; it must contribute to the strength and
perfection of the soul, to the elevation and progress
of the race.

And so I asked, was the wealth of this man all that
he possessed ? Had he no other claim to the respect
paid to him at his funeral than that he was rich ? I
do not refer to his Christian character, the most vital
test of a human being, because of that those religiously
associated with him can better judge; but I wish to
hold up to you the life of a man on the plane of successful business, — a life which was felt and recog-
nized as a power in the community. As I stood in
the great gathering, I turned to an aged man near me
and asked if he knew the deceased. With deep feeling
he replied, " I was his bookkeeper for many years and
I ought to know him well. He was the best friend i
ever had ; he did not wait for me to ask a kindness
but his ever-thoughtful, generous heart proffered aid
and the very aid I needed. He was a volunteer
bondsman, when I held a public office, and my wise
adviser." By another, who came from New Hamp
shire, I was told. " I have manufactured more thar
four million dollars' worth of goods for him, and neve

had a word of disagreement during twenty-two years."
I conversed with still another, who said, " Years since
I was unfortunate in business, and after paying one
hundred cents for every dollar of indebtedness, I
found myself with less than five hundred dollars to
commence the world anew. I was advised by friends
to go West. But how. I asked. can I get credit?
' Refer them to me,' said Mr. Dane. I went West,
taking with me twenty-five thousand dollars' worth
of goods. The winter following was one of unprec-
edented severity and hardship. I was greatly dis-
couraged, and wrote my friend that I could meet
all my payments on maturity but his. By the earliest
return mail I received this message : ' Let it stand
as long as you desire.' This," said the stranger,
" put fresh life into me, and I went to my work with
new hope and satisfaction. As the result of this act
of friendliness, I was able to pay my whole indebtedness on maturity except one thousand dollars, to my
dear old friend. But very soon I paid that, and the
winter's work was my new start in life."

You may remember that soon after the Great Fire
in Boston, in 1872, when the question arose as to
soliciting aid from abroad in behalf of the sufferers,
there came out in one of the daily papers of that
city a characteristic letter from Mr. Dane to this

effect: " Boston is a rich city; it has no occasion to solicit charity; its losses are immense, but it can sustain them. Let us take care of our own sufferers." Mr. Dane himself lost by the fire, and yet he closed his letter by subscribing one thousand dollars. Moved by this spirit, Boston undertook the great work of rebuilding her own wasted warehouses and relieving her own suffering poor.

Thus you see the difference between character and circumstances. The one is temporary, the other is lasting; the one drops from a man as our clothes drop from our limbs, the other inheres to a man in life and after death, and constitutes his only valid claim to remembrance. Of what consequence is it that a man is worth millions, if that is all that can be said about him? But it is a matter of consequence to the whole universe, to men and to angels and to God, that a man should be truthful, honest, and God-fearing. And, friends, we have fallen upon times when it is of the greatest urgency that practical righteousness should be emphasized and insisted upon. We ourselves are transient, — as the grass of the field we pass away. But there are great verities which stand out in life like the rocky headlands of our coast; these are the same yesterday, to-day, and forever.

In passing through our late civil war, our social life, in all its varied departments, was put to a fearful strain. Public virtue and religion, as well as business, civil order, and education, all felt the down-dragging influences of war. With it, there came in upon the people more expensive habits of living and an aversion to work and to economy. We are now passing through another change. We must go back to the former order of things. Men do not take kindly to this return ; multitudes would rather beg than work, and other multitudes, who scorn to beg, would rather steal than work. Persistent, steady application to employment has gone out of fashion. But it must be revived if the country is to be saved. Our young people must be taught, both by precept and example, that work is a divine calling, and absolutely essential to all true manhood and to all useful living.

It is with pleasure, therefore, that a note can be made of the life of a man who rose to wealth, position, and influence, not by some fortuitous speculation or by some fortunate turn of public affairs, but by his own honest and persevering toil, — a man whom neither the pursuit nor the possession of wealth tempted aside from duty.

OTHER PAPERS.

NEW ENGLAND SHOE AND LEATHER ASSOCIATION,
No. 125 FEDERAL STREET,
BOSTON, Aug. 2, 1875.

AT a meeting of the Shoe and Leather Dealers of Boston, held this day, to testify their respect for the late Francis Dane, the following resolutions were unanimously adopted : —

"*Resolved*, That the sudden death of Francis Dane, while it will be deeply felt in the many business circles in which he filled a useful and honorable position, brings especial grief to his associates in the Shoe and Leather trade, in whose ranks his native force and manliness and his thorough integrity had long given him a leading place ; and they feel it due to themselves, and to the young men who are coming up to take their places, to record their testimony to his many admirable traits of character.

"They recall the rare combination of energy and prudence that marked his business life. His was a mind of great breadth of view and firmness of grasp, ever eager to devise and bold to carry forward large enterprises, yet observant of details, and carrying with seeming ease the full memory of every minute particular. With thorough honesty of purpose he scorned every form of meanness or deceit.

"He freely shared with others the wealth which had crowned his labors, and his generosity ever prompted him to the largest hospitality and to a liberal support of every good work. The hearty friendliness of his broad, manly nature gave double value to his wise counsels and his ample gifts, and throughout the land, wherever his enterprise had made his name known, men will cherish among their most valued treasures the memory of that helpful kindliness and cheer which he carried into all his business intercourse.

"*Resolved*, That a committee of twelve be appointed to attend the funeral of our deceased friend, and that committee to consist of the following gentlemen: Thomas E. Proctor, L. B. Harrington, Miles

4

Washburn, Henry Poor, N. W. Rice, E. B. Phillips, John Cummings, A. J. Benyon, Albert Thompson, E. Marqueze, F. L. Fay, A. H. Batcheller, with as many others as can attend.

"*Resolved*, That our places of business shall be closed at 2 o'clock, P. M., and remain closed for the day.

"*Resolved*, That we tender our heartfelt sympathy to the widow and near relatives of our departed friend in their bereavement.

"*Resolved*, That a copy of these resolutions be presented to the family of the deceased."

THOMAS E. PROCTOR,
President.

CHARLES S. INGALLS,
Secretary.

SHOE AND LEATHER INSURANCE COMPANY,
52 DEVONSHIRE STREET,
BOSTON, Aug. 9, 1875.

AT a meeting of the Board of Directors held this day, the following resolutions were passed : —

"*Resolved*, That we have learned with deep regret the death of our friend and colleague, Mr. Francis Dane, and we desire to express our appreciation of his upright, manly, and honorable character, his integrity in business, his ready benevolence, his constant liberality, his unwearied efforts for the welfare of others ; and we offer our earnest and heartfelt sympathy to all the members of his bereaved family."

Very respectfully,

HENRY B. WHITE,
Secretary.

BOSTON SAFE DEPOSIT AND TRUST COMPANY,
POST OFFICE SQUARE, CORNER MILK AND CONGRESS STREETS,
BOSTON, Aug. 9, 1875.

"*Resolved*, That by the decease of Francis Dane the directors of this company have lost a most efficient co-worker and faithful friend, and that it is meet that they place on record some expression, however inadequate, of their estimate of his character and abilities.

Mr. Dane was a strong man, and made himself felt among all persons with whom he came in contact. He was whole-souled, benevolent in his

feelings, liberal in his gifts, and most hospitable. As a friend he was constant and untiring in his good offices. He detested meanness in all its forms, and by both precept and example did everything in his power to swell the numbers of the school of honorable merchants to which he belonged. As a merchant he was enterprising and energetic, yet cautious and painstaking. Endowed with an excellent memory, his knowledge of men and things made his services most valuable to the several monetary institutions with which he was identified ; and the directors, especially, realize that this institution, of which Mr. Dane was an active founder and a vice-president, has met with a great loss.

"*Resolved*. That the directors tender their heartfelt sympathy to the widow and relatives of the deceased in this their great affliction."

EDWARD P. BOND,
Secretary.

At the meeting of the Directors of the Warren National Bank, and a voluntary informal meeting of the Trustees of the Warren Five Cents Savings Bank, held conjointly, Monday, Aug. 2, Mr. Lewis Allen in the Chair, the death of Francis Dane having been announced, the following resolutions, prepared by a committee chosen by the meeting, were presented, viz. —

"*Resolved*, That on the decease of our late friend, former citizen and companion, Francis Dane, we cannot let the occasion pass without paying our humble tribute to his memory.

"He was a man of noble and most generous impulses : of broad, comprehensive views and capable of the successful working of them. He came among us some thirty-five or more years since, from his native town of Hamilton, without capital, without fame. Engaging in a small way as an individual manufacturer, by his talents, enlarging business capacity, his energy and enterprise, and especially by his integrity and large and generous heart, he won the respect and esteem of all with whom he had intercourse. His retentive memory of events, of matters great or small, was a remarkable characteristic of him. Such qualities soon placed him among us as one of the Directors of the Warren Bank, and one of the Trustees of the Warren Five Cents Savings Bank.

"We all can acknowledge the leading influence with which his judgment and opinion swayed us in business affairs, and the great regret we had in parting with him when such traits of character as he possessed called him to a larger sphere of enterprise and usefulness in the metropolis of our New England States.

As a citizen, although delicately and almost fastidiously withdrawing from prominence, he was foremost in devising and projecting for the good of the community, cheerfully and most liberally contributing from his acquisitions to promote every object which met his approval, and turning away from any meanness with indignant disgust. The void the death of so manly a man creates, the heart can feel but not express.

"*Resolved*, That our sympathies be tendered to the widow and relatives of the deceased in this home-touching bereavement.

"*Voted*, That these resolutions be adopted and entered upon the records of both institutions.

"*Voted*, That the two banks be closed at 12 M., in respect to the memory of Francis Dane.

"*Voted*, That a committee of four members from each bank attend the obsequies this day at Hamilton."

Attest,

F. C. MERRILL,
Secretary.

ESSEX AGRICULTURAL SOCIETY AT THE ANNUAL MEETING IN DANVERS, SEPT. 28, 1875.

When about to proceed to the election of officers, Allen W. Dodge, Esq., of Hamilton, requested permission to make a few remarks in relation to the late Francis Dane, Esq., of Hamilton. The speaker referred to Mr. Dane as a farmer who had for the last eight or ten years employed more farm-laborers than any other man in Essex County. In reply to a question as to his opinion whether farming paid, he replied, "I set down on one side all my expenses, upon the other all the health and happiness which I derive from the business, and when the balance is struck I find that farming pays." An average of the amount of premiums awarded to him during the eight years in which he had been an extensive contributor to the annual exhibitions showed that he had been entitled to about $55 per year, but he had never given a receipt for a single cent of this amount, but had invariably turned the whole sum into the treasury,— amounting to over $400. In closing, Mr. Dodge submitted the following resolutions, which were unanimously adopted : —

"*Resolved*, That the members of this Society have learned with deep regret of the recent and sudden death of their distinguished associate, Francis Dane, and would hereby record the expression of their profound sorrow at the great loss which they, in common with the community at large, have sustained.

"*Resolved*, That we shall ever retain a lively recollection of his many admirable traits of character, his genial manner, his public spirit, and his active interest in everything pertaining to farmers and the farm, — and especially of his inspiring presence at our annual gatherings and of his numerous and notable contributions to our public exhibitions.

"*Resolved*, That a copy of these resolutions be communicated to the family of our deceased associate."

BENJ. P. WARE, Pres.

CHARLES P. PRESTON, *Sec.*

THE RESOLUTION OF THE TRUSTEES OF DUMMER ACADEMY.

NEWBURYPORT, Oct. 18, 1875.

The trustees of Dummer Academy desire to place on record their appreciation of the loss they have sustained in the death of their late associate, Francis Dane. Although his connection with the Institution has been of comparatively recent date, yet the interest which he manifested in its success, and the suggestions he proposed for its advancement, impress his fellow trustees with the magnitude of the loss they have sustained. He was wise in council, of sound judgment, eminently practical, yet truly generous. We join with the large circle of his friends and relatives in mourning his loss.

JOHN PIKE, Pres.

S. J. SPALDING, *Sec.*

COPY OF MR. DANE'S LETTER REFERRED TO ON PAGES 21-22,
Published in the Daily Advertiser, Nov. 13, 1872.

RELIEF FROM ABROAD.

BOSTON, Nov. 16, 1872.

HON. WILLIAM GRAY,
Chairman Citizens' Relief Committee:

Dear Sir, — As a citizen and a sufferer, permit me to suggest that some earnest action be first taken among ourselves with reference to raising funds before appropriating the subscriptions from abroad so generously thrown upon us. Terrible as has been our calamity, it has not yet brought us to a position where we cannot aid and protect our suffering people. The truth is, a large proportion of our business community are

going to be greatly benefited by this disaster. Parties who escaped the fire will find their property largely enhanced in value; stores and buildings, long vacant, are being rented at high prices. Are these parties going to be backward at such times as this? Most assuredly not. In addition to this, the loss, great as it is, falls upon men who still have much left, and among the most valuable of their treasures preserved is their noble desire and purpose to extend the helping hand to the needy. We can but feel deeply grateful to the whole country for its sympathy and offers of aid, and should have no such pride as would prevent our accepting such offers, if circumstances made it necessary; but, with my views, I am unwilling to use the funds tendered until it appears that they are required. Let us first use our own subscriptions, and leave the appropriation of all others to await future developments.

As an earnest of my feelings in this matter, I herewith enclose my check for one thousand dollars, which, I believe, will be largely augmented, if it becomes known that first of all we are to do our duty in this matter.

Very respectfully yours,

FRANCIS DANE.

The following were among many notices of the funeral: —

FUNERAL OF THE LATE FRANCIS DANE.

The funeral services of the deceased were held at his late residence in Hamilton Monday afternoon. Probably five hundred relatives and friends were present, the 12.30 train from Boston alone conveying nearly two hundred ladies and gentlemen, among whom were the Committee of Twelve of the Boston Shoe and Leather Exchange, many members of that organization and officers of mercantile institutions with which the deceased had been connected. The warmth of the love which Mr. Dane had inspired during his life was shown in the grief which was expressed on all sides, not merely by those who had lived in intimacy with him, but by men who had known him only as a business man. The fine mansion upon which Mr. Dane had bestowed so much labor was filled with friends, and the grounds around for a hundred yards were crowded with carriages.

The remains rested in a handsome casket, which was covered with

flowers, and the placid, dead face was looked upon by hundreds of friends for the last time. Among the decorations was a magnificent floral harp, the tribute of Mr. William Emerson Baker, of Wellesley. There were handsome tributes also from Messrs. E. Marquize and Joseph Plummer. At 2.30 o'clock the religious services were commenced in the house. Prayer was offered by the Rev. Calvin Hill, of Hamilton, and then "Nearer, my God, to Thee" was sung by Mrs. Julia Houston West. She sang the words of the beautiful hymn with rare sweetness and pathos, and there could not have been a man or woman in the gathering who was not touched by them, coming at such a time. After the singing, the Rev. Edward Everett Hale of Boston read passages from the Scriptures, addressed the friends briefly, and offered a fervent prayer. In speaking of the deceased, Mr. Hale said that he never met him in the street without stopping him, even if it were but for a moment, because he always felt sure of hearing from him a word of faith, hope, or love. He said that the departed friend had always *lived* while he lived, not existed ; had lived for others as well as for himself, and in so doing had done his Master's work. After Mr. Hale's prayer the services closed with singing by Mrs. West.

After a delay of a few minutes the relatives and friends entered the carriages, which were nearly eighty in number. The pall-bearers were Messrs. John P. Robinson, Joseph Plummer, R. M. Pomeroy, and A. C. Mayhew of Boston, Oscar F. Whipple, Edwin A. Whipple, Wm. A. Brown, and Ira A. Dunnels of Hamilton. About four o'clock the remains were conveyed to the cemetery, which is about a mile from the late residence of the deceased. — *Boston Journal.*

THE LATE FRANCIS DANE.

The funeral of the late Francis Dane took place from the old family homestead in Hamilton yesterday afternoon. About noon the carriages of the numerous friends of the deceased began to arrive, and by two o'clock the grounds all around the house were thickly covered with hacks, carryalls, and other vehicles, which had borne hither a mourning multitude of friends. The body lay in the house in a little room off the sitting-room ; it was enclosed in a rich rosewood casket heavily mounted with silver.

The atmosphere of the apartment was heavy with the odor of the great floral designs which filled the room. Upon the foot of the coffin

rested a large and beautifully-arranged anchor, made of rosebuds and pinks, while near the head stood the symbolic harp of the broken string. Placed around the bier were crescents, stars, and baskets of rich and fragrant flowers eminently fitting to the occasion. The crescents were made of wheat and pinks. In the base of the floral heap was worked the words, " We shall meet again," and on the snowy top of the large flat bouquet was the word " Rest." The shoe and leather trade and the insurance and banking business were largely represented in the house. Prominent amongst these were Henry Poor, Esq., of Peabody; Edward Jacobs, Esq., Peabody; the officers of the Warren Bank, of Peabody: Stephen Blaney, Esq., Peabody; Lewis Allen, Esq., of Peabody. Nearly all these gentlemen belong to the Boston Board of Trade. Leonard Harrington, Esq., Salem; John A. Lord, Esq., Peabody; James Langley, Esq., and other prominent gentlemen were in the throng. Friends came by train and carriage from Peabody, Danvers, Salem, Lynn, Boston, and all over the State to attend this funeral. There were about seven hundred persons present, and more than a hundred carriages took places in the funeral procession. At two o'clock the house and verandas were crowded with spectators, representing all ranks of life and nearly every business and profession, and the funeral services were begun by an invocation by Rev. Mr. Hill, of Hamilton. Rev. Edward Everett Hale then offered a fervent prayer, and read appropriate Scriptural selections. These were interspersed with solos sung by Mrs. Julia Houston West. The funeral procession then formed, and the remains were conveyed to the cemetery, near the church, and placed in the family tomb. The following named gentlemen acted as pall-bearers: John P. Robinson, A. C. Mayhew, R. M. Pomeroy, and Joseph Plummer. The friends left the graveyard after performing the last rites over their beloved associate and fellow-citizen, and slowly dispersing went towards their homes. — *Boston Post.*

GENEALOGY.

THE following Genealogy of the Dane Family was drawn up by Perley Derby, Esq., of Salem, Mass., July, 1871 : —

JOHN DANE was born in England about 1587. His will, made Sept. 7, 1658, and proved Oct. 16, 1658, is on file in the Probate Office, Boston. According to the " Narrative " written by his son John, he lived first at Berkhampstead, England, where he probably was born, and removed thence to Bishop's Stortford, Herts. While in England he followed the occupation of a tailor, was devoutly pious, and a strict disciplinarian in matters pertaining to morals and religion, which example he rigidly enforced upon his children. He married twice. His first wife, a very pious woman (name and date of marriage unknown), was at one time servant to Lady Margaret Denny, who was maid of honor to Queen Elizabeth and wife to Sir Edward Denny, groom of the queen's privy chamber. Lady Margaret died April, 1648, aged 88. Mr. Dane, prompted by the example of his son John, who preceded him shortly before, emigrated to Massachusetts about 1636 wife, son Francis, and daughter Elizabeth. He first went to Ipswich, where his son John was then living, and had a house-lot granted him April, 1639, in the street called the West End, on the north side of Ipswich River. Here he lived till about 1641-2, when he removed to Roxbury, where his wife shortly after died, and he married for his second wife, 1643, Annis, widow of William Chandler, who came from England to Roxbury in 1637, with his wife and four children, and died June 19, 1641. Under date of Feb. 2, 1651-2, he makes a deed of gift to his "dear and loving wife, Annis Dane, formerly wife of William Chandler, all the housing and lands that were said Chandler's." After the decease of her husband, Mrs. Dane

5

married for the third time, 1661, John, son of John Parminter, of Sudbury, who died April 12, 1666. Children : —

> *Elizabeth*[2]. b. ——, in England : d. in Ipswich, Jan. 21, 1663 ; m. James How, who died May 17, 1702.
>
> ▸ JOHN[2]. b. in England about 1613.
>
> *Francis*[2]. b. in England, 1616. It is said he came to New England with Rev. Nathaniel Rogers, and arrived in Boston November, 1636. Settled first in Ipswich ; removed to Andover, 1648, and was second minister of that place. He died Feb. 17, 1698-9, aged 82. He married 1st, Elizabeth Ingalls, of Lynn ; m. 2d, widow Mary Thomas, who died Feb. 18, 1684 ; m. 3d, widow Hannah Abbott, b. 1629 ; d. June 2, 1711.

JOHN[2]. b. in England about 1613 ; came to Roxbury about 1635, thence to Ipswich, where he d. Sept. 20, 1684 ; Surgeon ; m. 1st, Eleanor Clark ; m. 2d, Alice ——, who after his decease m. Jeremiah Meacham of Salem. Children : —

> *Mary*[3]. b. about 1636 : d. May 10, 1679 ; m. Aug. 24, 1658, William Chandler of Andover.
>
> JOHN[3]. b. in Ipswich about 1644.
>
> *Sarah*[3]. b. about 1645 : d. Dec. 28, 1702 : m. Sept. 23, 1668, Daniel Warner, Jr., of Ipswich, b. 1640, d. Nov. 24, 1699.
>
> *Philemon*[3]. b. about 1646 : d. Oct. 18, 1716 : joined the church Feb. 8, 1673-4 ; physician ; m. 1st, Oct. 7, 1685, Mary Thomson ; m. 2d, Dec. 25, 1690, Ruth Convers, who d. Jan. 12, 1735-6.
>
> *Rebecca*[3]. b. —— ; d. —— ; m. James Hovey.
>
> *Elizabeth*[3]. b. —— : d. —— ; m. Reginald Foster, Jr., b. in England, d. in Chebacco Parish, Ipswich, Dec. 28, 1707.

JOHN[3]. b. in Ipswich about 1644 : d. Jan. 1707-8 ; he lived at the Hamlet, where he sold to the town, 1705, one half acre of land for a burial-place. In 1692 he was a juror in witchcraft cases ; yeoman ; m. Dec. 27, 1671, Abigail Warner. Children : —

> *Abigail*[4]. b. Dec. 15, 1673 ; m. March 27, 1705, Joseph Crackbone of Cambridge.
>
> *Rebecca*[4]. b. Sept. 18, 1676.
>
> *Elizabeth*[4]. b. March 6, 1678-9.
>
> JOHN[4]. b. Nov. 29, 1681.
>
> *Susannah*[4]. b. March 6, 1685-6 ; buried March 24, 1687.

35

Daniel, b. about 1689: d. Jan. 22, 1730: yeoman: m. 1st, March 1?, 1714, Lydia Day, b. Oct. 27, 1694; m. 2d, Mary Annable.

Nathaniel, b. June 27, 1691; d. June, 1760; published Dec. 6, 1712, to Elizabeth Porter, b. Nov. 17, 1694; m. 2d, March, 1716-17, Anna Low, who d. Feb. 1730-31: m. 3d, Dec. 23, 1732, Esther Kimball of Wenham, b. April 1, 1698.

John, b. Nov. 29, 1681; d. at the Hamlet, May 22, 1755: yeoman; m. Martha ——, who was received to the church in Hamlet, Dec. 1722. Children :—

> *John*, baptized April 22, 1716; d. April, 1796: published May 8, 1761, to widow Ednah Patch, b. 1735; d. April 5, 1814, aged 79.
>
> *Martha*, baptized May 10, 1718.
>
> *Abigail*, baptized Jan. 24, 1719-20.
>
> *Elizabeth*, baptized July 16, 1721; d. ——; m. April 6, 1742, to James Adams.
>
> *Joseph*, baptized Feb. 2, 1723-24; probably removed to North Brookfield.
>
> William⁵, b. Aug. 1725.
>
> *Benjamin*, b. May, 1728; d. Nov. 1756; published Aug. 29, 1755, to Mary Cogswell.
>
> *Sarah*, b. July, 1730.
>
> *Daniel*, b. March, 1733; d. June, 1735.
>
> *Lydia*, b. Aug., 1735; d. Sept. 17, 1748.

William⁵, b. Aug. 1725; removed 1762 to North Brookfield, where he l. March 2, 1825, aged 99 years, 7 months; yeoman; published May 13, 1748, to Sarah Stone, of Ipswich, b. 1724, d. Aug. 24, 1806, aged 82. Children : —

> John⁶, b. May 22, 1750.
>
> *Benjamin⁶*, b. ——; d. ——; removed from North Brookfield to Shutesbury.
>
> *Joseph⁶*, b. 1752: d. March 25, 1814; lived in West Brookfield; m. Lucy Gilbert.
>
> *William⁶*, b. 1754; d. April 22, 1825: m. Lydia Kendrick of North Brookfield: d. Aug. 14, 1817.
>
> *Judith⁶*, b. 1758; d. Nov. 1, 1821: m. 1775, Jason Bigelow, b. 1754; d. Feb. 2, 1826.
>
> *Sarah⁶*, b. 1761: d. April 12, 1844; m. 1777 Joseph Waite, of North Brookfield.
>
> *Martha⁶*, b. ——; d. ——; m. Jacob Gilbert, of North Brookfield.

JOHN[5], b. May 22, 1750; d. Dec. 22, 1842; yeoman; m. 1st, about 1778, widow Dinah Patch, b. 1757; d. Jan. 12, 1792; published, 2d, Dec. 29, 1791, to Eunice Patch, b. 1757; d. July 25, 1843. Children: —

    Dinah, baptized Feb. 27, 1780; d. Oct. 22, 1794.

    JOHN[6], b. Jan. 12, 1782.

JOHN[6], b. Jan. 12, 1782; d. June 16, 1821; yeoman; m. Fanny Quarles, b. May 24, 1784; d. March 28, 1866. Children: —

    George, b. June 24, 1804; m. Dec. 19, 1824, Mary Annable, b. March 20, 1801; she d. Aug. 12, 1873.

    Ednah, b. May 12, 1806; m. Nov. 11, 1833, Dudley Porter, Jr.; he d. June 22, 1856; she d. Dec. 11, 1872.

    Fanny Quarles, b. Aug. 5, 1808; d. Oct. 27, 1825.

    Mary Ann, b. Aug. 4, 1810.

    Jerusha Quarles, b. Aug. 25, 1812; m. Aug. 4, 1839, Daniel S. Henderson; she d. April 24, 1868.

    John, b. April 15, 1815; m. April 30, 1839, Lydia E. Sceggle, b. Jan. 2, 1820.

    Samuel, b. June 14, 1817; m. 1st, Mary A. Barker, b. 1816, d. March 28, 1844; m. 2d, June 3, 1845, Martha Whipple, b. Feb. 23, 1815.

    FRANCIS[8], b. Aug. 6, 1819; d. July 30, 1875.

    William Augustus, b. Aug. 7, 1822; m. June 5, 1845, Almira Whipple, b. Aug. 7, 1822.

    Joseph Felt, b. Sept. 25, 1825; m. Feb. 24, 1853, Caroline E. Marks, b. Jan. 13, 1830.

    Fanny, b. Oct. 9, 1828; m. April 26, 1846, Andrew Story, 2d, of Essex.

FRANCIS[7], b. Aug. 6, 1819; d. July 30, 1875; m. Oct. 10, 1842, Zerviah Brown, of Hamilton, b. Feb. 1, 1819.

www.ingramcontent.com/pod-product-compliance
Lightning Source LLC
Chambersburg PA
CBHW030716110426
42739CB00030B/600